COVER TO COVER

31 DAYS FOR **ADVENT**
FOR SMALL GROUP OR PERSONAL USE

D0680174

Journey
TO
Christmas

CWR 🌀 **24-7 PRAYER**

Pete Greig, Carla Harding, Phil Togwell and Jill Weber

Contents

About the authors

Pete Greig is a best-selling author, pastor and bewildered instigator of the 24-7 Prayer movement, which has reached more than half the nations on earth. He is also the Senior Pastor of Emmaus Road Church in Guildford, an Ambassador for the NGO Tearfund, and teaches at St Mellitus Theological College in London. For seven years, Pete served with the senior leadership team at HTB and Alpha International. His publications include *Red Moon Rising, God on Mute, The Prayer Course, Dirty Glory* and *How to Pray.* He loves art galleries, live music and knocking down walls.

Carla Harding is the National Director for 24-7 Prayer Great Britain. Her life was hijacked by God in 1999 during a two-hour stint in the first 24-7 Prayer Room. Carla lives in Chichester with her husband Steve and their two children. She loves prayer and worship, friends and food, a well-told story, international adventures and a challenge to get her teeth into. In her spare time, Carla is an active member of Revelation Church and the lead singer of a band.

Phil Togwell lives on the north-east coast of England with his family (one wife, three daughters, two dogs). Phil trained and worked in a wide range of youth and community settings before serving as 24-7 Prayer's UK Director for seven years. He now leads 24-7's Prayer Spaces in Schools teams, which help equip Christians to serve the spiritual and pastoral life of their local schools. Phil also serves the Anglican Diocese of Durham's Prayer Project and Missional Leadership for Growth programmes.

Jill Weber is married to Kirk and they have one daughter. Before moving to the UK in 2018, Jill was the Abbess of a 24-7 New Monastic Community in Canada for 17 years. Jill serves 24-7 Prayer as International Director of Houses of Prayer, and is Director of Spiritual Formation at Emmaus Road Church in Guildford. She is the Global Convenor of the Order of the Mustard Seed, a lay ecumenical religious order. A trained spiritual director and writer, Jill is passionate about helping others to be awake and responsive to the presence and activity of God in their lives.

INTRODUCTION

Every December, Christians all over the world intentionally embark on an Advent journey towards the day we celebrate the Son of God becoming flesh and blood and moving into the neighbourhood (John 1:14, *The Message*). This journey may not be physical, but hopefully it's a travelling of the heart, mind and soul closer to hope, closer to gratitude, and closer to Jesus.

This Advent we offer you some travelling companions. Journey with us – four leaders from the 24-7 Prayer movement – and journey with key characters from the Christmas story. Together we'll meditate on Scripture and P.R.A.Y. our way through December.

Each day, we will:
Pause – stilling ourselves and connecting with God
Rejoice and Reflect – giving thanks and engaging with short passages of Scripture
Ask – bringing our questions and needs to the Lord
Yield – surrendering ourselves to God's will in our lives

Inspired by Christian heroes and traditions throughout the centuries, we've written prayers we'll be returning to daily, we'll be making space for *Selah* (opportunities to pause, reflect and respond), and we'll be reading each passage from the Bible at least twice to help us listen closely to what God is saying to us through His Word.

Each reflection is written not to be read through quickly, but to be prayed through slowly, giving space for Scripture and the Holy Spirit to speak. So take your time – you could even try journalling in response to each question or opportunity to pray.

As we set off towards the celebration of Christ's birth together, our prayer is that you would encounter Jesus every step of the journey.

Pete Greig, Carla Harding, Phil Togwell and Jill Weber

DAY 1: ADVENT SUNDAY

Today is Advent Sunday. This is the beginning of our journey to Christmas.

Busyness, not rest, is perhaps the word we would most likely use to describe the season of Advent. The shopping, parties, decoration and plans can make the month of December fly by in a blur of tinsel and turkey. Let's embrace this Sabbath beginning as an opportunity to take rest; to change pace this Advent.

Most days we'll be pausing, meditating on the Bible, asking questions and yielding to God's will in our lives. But once a week, starting today, we'll be praying a little differently.

Join us in praying this Sabbath prayer...

As we journey towards Christmas, let us prepare our hearts for Christ's coming.

One of the earliest recorded prayers of the Church is the Aramaic word *maranatha*, which literally means, 'Come, Lord Jesus'. The Latin word *adventus* means the same thing – 'come'. This is a season of waiting and wanting; looking and longing; inviting Christ to come once more into our lives and into our world. Pause now and repeat this ancient prayer several times slowly:

Maranatha, come, Lord Jesus.

— Selah

We're going to stick with this simple prayer, *Maranatha*, a bit longer.

If you are aware of sinful thoughts, words or deeds in your life, acknowledge them now before the Lord, praying: *Maranatha, come, Lord Jesus.*

— Selah

Now think of someone who needs Christ's love today, praying for them: *Maranatha, come, Lord Jesus.*

— Selah

Next, remember your own local church and the many activities it has planned during this Christmas season, praying again: *Maranatha, come, Lord Jesus.*

— Selah

Finally, think of a place in the world that desperately needs Christ's comfort today, praying: *Maranatha, come, Lord Jesus.*

— Selah

In the twelfth century, Saint Bernard of Clairvaux, a forerunner of the Cistercian order of monks, notably said that Christ comes three times: in the past to Bethlehem at Christmas, in the future at the end of the age, and in the present day lives of believers. Let's pray for all three:

> *Thank You, Father, for loving us so much that You sent Your Son*
> *to save us.*
> *Maranatha. May Jesus be born again among us this Christmas.*
> *Thank You, Jesus, that You came before and You are coming*
> *again in glory.*
> *Maranatha. We long for You to return and make all things new.*
> *Thank You, Holy Spirit, for filling my life.*
> *Maranatha. May the Lord Jesus Christ be born again in me today.*

Blessing

May this day bring Sabbath rest to your heart and your home.

May your peace and perspective be renewed in the busyness of this season.

May your hand be free enough from spending and acquiring to receive God's gift.

May a little of the wonder of Christmas awaken the child within today.

May God's Word feed you and His Spirit lead you into the week and into the life to come.

WEEK ONE

Journeying with
Elizabeth and Zechariah

JILL WEBER

DAY 2

This is the second day of our journey towards Christmas. Each day we will PAUSE. We will REJOICE and REFLECT on Scripture. We will ASK God to help us and others, and we will YIELD to God's will.

This month we will follow the stories of the characters caught up in the drama of Jesus' birth. This week we accompany Jesus' relatives, Elizabeth and Zechariah.

PAUSE

I pause now, breathe deeply, and re-centre my scattered senses on the presence of God.

— Selah

Lord, in this busy season, please help me to be still. I am opening my ears now to hear amazing things from You, quietly preparing my heart for the wonder of Your coming at Christmas.

REJOICE and REFLECT

What about God am I most grateful for today? I tell Him now.

Christmas is often associated with joy and peace, but our journey begins somewhere unexpected – the wilderness. Today we're reflecting on a prophecy in Isaiah 40. In this passage, the prophet heralds the coming of Elizabeth and Zechariah's son, John the Baptist, and predicts how his voice will prepare hearts to recognise and receive Jesus.

'A voice of one calling:
"In the wilderness prepare
the way for the LORD;
make straight in the desert
a highway for our God.
Every valley shall be raised up,
every mountain and hill made low;

the rough ground shall become level,
the rugged places a plain."' **Isaiah 40:3–4**

Christmas is a time of celebration, but we might not always experience it that way. Regardless of the season, we sometimes have low valleys of discouragement and disappointment, and struggle with obstacles that seem like mountains.

ASK

What is the landscape of my wilderness right now? What are my valleys, my low places? What are my mountains, my obstacles? God, how can You make the rough ground of my life level?

— Selah

Who do I know who is struggling, discouraged and disappointed? Do I have friends who are wandering in the desert? God, I pray for them right now.

— Selah

YIELD

As I return to the passage, I open my ears to hear Your Word at a deeper level, and my heart to yield to Your will once again.

'A voice of one calling:
"In the wilderness prepare
the way for the LORD;
make straight in the desert
a highway for our God.
Every valley shall be raised up,
every mountain and hill made low;
the rough ground shall become level,
the rugged places a plain."' **Isaiah 40:3–4**

In the wilderness, John the Baptist finds his voice. Among the valleys and the mountains, he is forged as a messenger who prepares people to recognise and receive Jesus.

Who could I be a messenger to this Advent?

— Selah

Jesus, I yield to Your wilderness work in me. As I become familiar with the contours of my own personal desert, help me find my voice and become a trustworthy guide for others.

Closing Prayer

Father, may I live this day, true to You, come what may.
Jesus, may I give this day, in kindness to all, in every way.
Spirit, may I love this day, proclaiming Christ in all I say.
Amen.

DAY 3

This is the third day of our journey together towards Christmas.

PAUSE

I pause now, breathe deeply, and re-centre my scattered senses on the presence of God.

— Selah

Lord, in this busy season, please help me to be still. I am opening my ears now to hear amazing things from You, quietly preparing my heart for the wonder of Your coming at Christmas.

REJOICE and REFLECT

What about God am I most grateful for today? I tell Him now.

The Advent story in Luke culminates in the birth of Jesus, but begins with the story of Mary's cousins, Elizabeth and Zechariah. They come from a good family. They have a good reputation. They have obeyed and served faithfully for a long time. And yet there is a hole in the middle of their lives.

'In the time of Herod king of Judea there was a priest named Zechariah, who belonged to the priestly division of Abijah; his wife Elizabeth was also a descendant of Aaron. Both of them were righteous in the sight of God, observing all the Lord's commands and decrees blamelessly. But they were childless because Elizabeth was not able to conceive, and they were both very old.' **Luke 1:5–7**

We enter into Elizabeth's and Zechariah's story in the low place of infertility. The obstacle of advanced age. The experience of disappointment and hope deferred. There are parts of our lives that we allow the world to see – often the most presentable parts. But on the inside, each of us carries disappointment or regret at times.

ASK

I ask myself, are there places in my life where I have obeyed and served faithfully, without seeming to have anything to show for my obedience? God, I hold my disappointment and regret before You, and wait for You with hope this Christmas.

— Selah

I think of those I know who have served and obeyed, and are still waiting. I bring them before You now. In particular I pray for those who can't have children. I pray for them now: may the God of all hope give them joy and peace as they trust in You, that they would abound in hope by the power of the Holy Spirit, even as they wait (Rom. 15:13).

— Selah

13

YIELD

As I return to the passage, I open my ears to hear Your Word at a deeper level, and my heart to yield to Your will once again.

'In the time of Herod king of Judea there was a priest named Zechariah, who belonged to the priestly division of Abijah; his wife Elizabeth was also a descendant of Aaron. Both of them were righteous in the sight of God, observing all the Lord's commands and decrees blamelessly. But they were childless because Elizabeth was not able to conceive, and they were both very old.' **Luke 1:5–7**

Not only were Zechariah and Elizabeth childless, but they were also very old – well beyond childbearing years. There was a window of opportunity and it had passed them by. Life had moved forward and left them behind.

Do I feel like I've missed a window of God's opportunity? That I've missed the boat, been left behind?

— Selah

God, it's tempting to rush to the end of the story – 'and they all lived happily ever after.' But I want to be honest about my disappointment, perplexity and lament. God, I hold before You the problems that seem unsolvable, and I'm trusting You whether You answer my prayers or not.

Closing Prayer

Father, may I live this day, true to You, come what may.
Jesus, may I give this day, in kindness to all, in every way.
Spirit, may I love this day, proclaiming Christ in all I say.
Amen.

DAY 4

It is the first week of Advent. Together we are following various people in the biblical story as they journey towards Christmas.

PAUSE

I pause now, breathe deeply, and re-centre my scattered senses on the presence of God.

— Selah

Lord, in this busy season, please help me to be still. I am opening my ears now to hear amazing things from You, quietly preparing my heart for the wonder of Your coming at Christmas.

REJOICE and REFLECT

What about God am I most grateful for today? I tell Him now.

This week, we accompany Jesus' relatives, Elizabeth and Zechariah. Yesterday we joined them in their disappointment and yearning. Today we meet Zechariah in the temple. It is business as usual: he is attending to his regular religious routine, and all of a sudden the unexpected happens. Let's reflect on Luke 1 together.

> 'Then an angel of the Lord appeared to him, standing at the right side of the altar of incense. When Zechariah saw him, he was startled and was gripped with fear. But the angel said to him: "Do not be afraid, Zechariah; your prayer has been heard. Your wife Elizabeth will bear you a son, and you are to call him John."'
> **Luke 1:11–13**

'Your prayer has been heard,' the angel says to Zechariah. Our prayers have been heard. They never disappear. God collects every single one of them. In Psalm 56:8 (NLT), the psalmist affirms:

'You keep track of all my sorrows.
You have collected all my tears in your bottle.
You have recorded each one in your book.'

ASK

*'Your prayer has been heard.' How do I feel when I hear that sentence?
What have I been believing for, bringing to God and waiting for – for a
long time? I name them in quiet before You, Lord. And after each one,
I say to myself, 'My prayer has been heard.'*

— Selah

*God, bring encouragement to all those I know who have been praying,
believing and waiting for a long time. I name them before You. May
they know that their prayers have been heard.*

— Selah

YIELD

*As I return to the passage, I open my ears to hear Your Word at a
deeper level, and my heart to yield to Your will once again.*

'Then an angel of the Lord appeared to him, standing at the right
side of the altar of incense. When Zechariah saw him, he was
startled and was gripped with fear. But the angel said to him:
"Do not be afraid, Zechariah; your prayer has been heard. Your
wife Elizabeth will bear you a son, and you are to call him John."'
Luke 1:11–13

The name 'John' means 'God has been gracious – has shown favour'.
One of the meanings of the word 'gracious' in the Scriptures is 'to show
kindness'. It is in God's nature to respond to our hopes and needs with
graciousness and kindness.

How can I, unapologetically and with an open heart, receive His goodness?

— Selah

God, in this Advent season, I recognise Your gracious nature and I and yield to Your kindness towards me. You are my gift this Christmas and I receive You.

Closing Prayer

Father, may I live this day, true to You, come what may.
Jesus, may I give this day, in kindness to all, in every way.
Spirit, may I love this day, proclaiming Christ in all I say.
Amen.

DAY 5

It is the first week of Advent.

PAUSE

I pause now, breathe deeply, and re-centre my scattered senses on the presence of God.

— Selah

Lord, in this busy season, please help me to be still. I am opening my ears now to hear amazing things from You, quietly preparing my heart for the wonder of Your coming at Christmas.

REJOICE and REFLECT

What about God am I most grateful for today? I tell Him now.

Today we continue our journey with Elizabeth and Zechariah. Zechariah is in the temple, offering up prayers to God, when he has a surprise encounter with an angel. Let's reflect on the angel's message.

'He will be a joy and delight to you, and many will rejoice because of his birth, for he will be great in the sight of the Lord. He is never to take wine or other fermented drink, and he will be filled with the Holy Spirit even before he is born. He will bring back many of the people of Israel to the Lord their God. And he will go on before the Lord, in the spirit and power of Elijah, to turn the hearts of the parents to their children and the disobedient to the wisdom of the righteous – to make ready a people prepared for the Lord.' **Luke 1:14–17**

Finally Zechariah and Elizabeth's prayer is being answered, and with it comes the promise of joy and delight. If we're honest, our attitude towards answered prayer can sometimes be indifference, ingratitude or entitlement: 'Well, God, it took You long enough!' But when we take God's goodness for granted we tend to miss out on the joy and delight of celebration.

ASK

What was the last prayer God answered for me? How did my heart respond? Lord, I ask Your forgiveness for the times when I haven't fully appreciated Your kindness to me.

— Selah

God, would You dismantle our culture of entitlement and ingratitude, especially as it can be heightened at Christmas time. Lord, I pray for my church. Help us to resist this culture and act in the opposite spirit. May our community be characterised by gratitude, delight and joy.

— Selah

YIELD

As I return to the passage, I open my ears to hear Your Word at a deeper level, and my heart to yield to Your will once again.

'He will be a joy and delight to you, and many will rejoice because of his birth, for he will be great in the sight of the Lord. He is never to take wine or other fermented drink, and he will be filled with the Holy Spirit even before he is born. He will bring back many of the people of Israel to the Lord their God. And he will go on before the Lord, in the spirit and power of Elijah, to turn the hearts of the parents to their children and the disobedient to the wisdom of the righteous – to make ready a people prepared for the Lord.' **Luke 1:14–17**

God answers Zechariah and Elizabeth's prayer for their own sake, to give them joy. But God also has bigger plans – plans for a whole people – to bring them back to Himself.

When the Lord fulfils His promises to me and answers my prayers, it is rarely just for me alone. Blessing also spills over to the lives of those around me.

— Selah

God, I give myself to joy; to delight. As I receive from You, may I share Your love, Your grace and Your redemption to all those around me.

Closing Prayer
Father, may I live this day, true to You, come what may.
Jesus, may I give this day, in kindness to all, in every way.
Spirit, may I love this day, proclaiming Christ in all I say.
Amen.

DAY 6

It is the first week of Advent.

PAUSE

I pause now, breathe deeply, and re-centre my scattered senses on the presence of God.

— Selah

Lord, in this busy season, please help me to be still. I am opening my ears now to hear amazing things from You, quietly preparing my heart for the wonder of Your coming at Christmas.

REJOICE and REFLECT

What about God am I most grateful for today? I tell Him now.

Over the last few days of our journey towards Christmas, we've been reflecting on Zechariah's encounter with an angel. Now we join his wife, Elizabeth, as she has her own divine encounter. She has received a promise and conceived a child. About six months into her pregnancy, she has a visitor – her cousin, Mary, who is also newly pregnant.

> 'When Elizabeth heard Mary's greeting, the baby leaped in her womb, and Elizabeth was filled with the Holy Spirit. In a loud voice she exclaimed: "Blessed are you among women, and blessed is the child you will bear! But why am I so favoured, that the mother of my Lord should come to me? As soon as the sound of your greeting reached my ears, the baby in my womb leaped for joy.' **Luke 1:41–44**

When Mary visits Elizabeth, something unusual happens. Elizabeth is filled with the Holy Spirit and her baby leaps within her womb. Deep inside, Elizabeth knows that God has done something special in Mary. Full of the Holy Spirit, Elizabeth recognises the dream of God planted deep inside Mary. She recognises what God has done – she sees it and names it.

ASK

Have I ever experienced a gut response to the presence or activity of the Holy Spirit? When have my heart, soul and body known something before my mind has caught up? God, help me to be sensitive to Your movements within me.

— *Selah*

God, I pray for Your Church, that we would be filled with the Holy Spirit so that we can recognise and celebrate what You are doing in others.

— *Selah*

YIELD

As I return to the passage, I open my ears to hear Your Word at a deeper level, and my heart to yield to Your will once again.

'When Elizabeth heard Mary's greeting, the baby leaped in her womb, and Elizabeth was filled with the Holy Spirit. In a loud voice she exclaimed: "Blessed are you among women, and blessed is the child you will bear! But why am I so favoured, that the mother of my Lord should come to me? As soon as the sound of your greeting reached my ears, the baby in my womb leaped for joy.' **Luke 1:41–44**

A beautiful part of this story is that after Mary is seen, named and affirmed, she then sings one of the most beautiful hymns of all time: the *Magnificat*. When we are seen, named and affirmed – when others see the dreams of God planted deep inside of us – often we are released to respond to God in worship.

I yield myself to You, Holy Spirit. Come and fill me. Show me Your hidden work in others and so that I might see it, name it and bless it.

Closing Prayer

Father, may I live this day, true to You, come what may.
Jesus, may I give this day, in kindness to all, in every way.
Spirit, may I love this day, proclaiming Christ in all I say.
Amen.

DAY 7

It is the first week of Advent.

PAUSE

I pause now, breathe deeply, and re-centre my scattered senses on the presence of God.

— Selah

Lord, in this busy season, please help me to be still. I am opening my ears now to hear amazing things from You, quietly preparing my heart for the wonder of Your coming at Christmas.

REJOICE and REFLECT

What about God am I most grateful for today? I tell Him now.

This is our final day of our journey with Zechariah and Elizabeth towards Christmas. Today we read of their baby, John, being dedicated in the temple. In Jewish culture, the blessing of the father is the most valuable heritage they pass on to their children. In this passage, let's reflect on Zechariah's blessing for his son.

'And you, my child, will be called a prophet of the Most High;
  for you will go on before the Lord to prepare the way for him,

to give his people the knowledge of salvation
through the forgiveness of their sins,
because of the tender mercy of our God,
by which the rising sun will come to us from heaven
to shine on those living in darkness
and in the shadow of death,
to guide our feet into the path of peace.' **Luke 1:76–79**

Zechariah's song is not only a personal blessing for his son, but it also positions John in the larger story of God that is unfolding: God's plan to redeem His people, Israel, and all of humanity by sending His only Son, Jesus.

ASK

Have words of blessing been spoken over me? What are they? In this time of quiet, I remember them and thank God for them.

— Selah

In Zechariah's song, he mentions those in need of salvation. Who do I know who is living in darkness and in the shadow of death? I name them. Lord, I ask You to shine on them. Guide them onto the path of peace. May they receive the gift of Jesus this Christmas.

— Selah

YIELD

As I return to the passage, I open my ears to hear Your Word at a deeper level, and my heart to yield to Your will once again.

'And you, my child, will be called a prophet of the Most High;
for you will go on before the Lord to prepare the way for him,
to give his people the knowledge of salvation
through the forgiveness of their sins,
because of the tender mercy of our God,

by which the rising sun will come to us from heaven
to shine on those living in darkness
and in the shadow of death,
to guide our feet into the path of peace.' **Luke 1:76–79**

John was blessed to be a blessing. In the same way, we are blessed by God to be a blessing to others. Our story is not ours alone, but it is embedded in the larger story of God's rescue and redemption of everyone and everything.

God, I receive every blessing You have for me, knowing that those blessings are not for me alone but to be shared with others. I give myself to You, that I might be a part of Your rescue and redemption story.

Closing Prayer
Father, may I live this day, true to You, come what may.
Jesus, may I give this day, in kindness to all, in every way.
Spirit, may I love this day, proclaiming Christ in all I say.
Amen.

DAY 8

Today is the second Sunday of Advent. As today is the Sabbath, we'll be deliberately interrupting our Monday to Saturday rhythm and praying a little differently. Join us in praying this Sabbath prayer...

As we journey towards Christmas, let us prepare our hearts for Christ's coming.

One of the earliest recorded prayers of the Church is the Aramaic word *maranatha*, which literally means, 'Come, Lord Jesus'. The Latin word *adventus* means the same thing – 'come'. This is a season of waiting and wanting; looking and longing; inviting Christ to come once more into our lives and into our world. Pause now and repeat this ancient prayer several times slowly:

Maranatha, come, Lord Jesus.

— Selah

We're going to stick with this simple prayer, *Maranatha*, a bit longer.

If you are aware of sinful thoughts, words or deeds in your life, acknowledge them now before the Lord, praying: *Maranatha, come, Lord Jesus.*

— Selah

Now think of someone who needs Christ's love today, praying for them: *Maranatha, come, Lord Jesus.*

— Selah

Next, remember your own local church and the many activities it has planned during this Christmas season, praying again: *Maranatha, come, Lord Jesus.*

— Selah

Finally, think of a place in the world that desperately needs Christ's comfort today, praying: *Maranatha, come, Lord Jesus.*

— Selah

In the twelfth century, Saint Bernard of Clairvaux, a forerunner of the Cistercian order of monks, notably said that Christ comes three times: in the past to Bethlehem at Christmas, in the future at the end of the age, and in the present day lives of believers. Let's pray for all three:

Thank You, Father, for loving us so much that You sent Your Son to save us.
Maranatha. May Jesus be born again among us this Christmas.
Thank You, Jesus, that You came before and You are coming

again in glory.
Maranatha. We long for You to return and make all things new.
Thank You, Holy Spirit, for filling my life.
Maranatha. May the Lord Jesus Christ be born again in me today.

Blessing

May this day bring Sabbath rest to your heart and your home.

May your peace and perspective be renewed in the busyness of this season.

May your hand be free enough from spending and acquiring to receive God's gift.

May a little of the wonder of Christmas awaken the child within today.

May God's Word feed you and His Spirit lead you into the week and into the life to come.

WEEK TWO

Journeying with Mary

CARLA HARDING

DAY 9

This week, in the season of Advent, we are exploring the journey of Jesus' mother, Mary.

PAUSE

I pause now, breathe deeply, and re-centre my scattered senses on the presence of God.

— Selah

Lord, in this busy season, please help me to be still. I am opening my ears now to hear amazing things from You, quietly preparing my heart for the wonder of Your coming at Christmas.

REJOICE and REFLECT

What about God am I most grateful for today? I tell Him now.

Today we reflect on the words of Isaiah – words that foreshadow the birth of Jesus and God's plan for Mary, Jesus' mother. The prophecy comes in the middle of a conversation between King Ahaz and God. The king is facing invasion and God is offering a sign of hope...

> 'Again the LORD spoke to Ahaz, "Ask the LORD your God for a sign, whether in the deepest depths or in the highest heights." But Ahaz said, "I will not ask; I will not put the LORD to the test." Then Isaiah said, "Hear now, you house of David! Is it not enough to try the patience of humans? Will you try the patience of my God also? Therefore the Lord himself will give you a sign: the virgin will conceive and give birth to a son, and will call him Immanuel."' **Isaiah 7:10–14**

King Ahaz is in trouble. Not one but two kings are coming for his throne. Why doesn't he ask for a sign? Why doesn't he look for hope and reassurance?

At first glance his response seems respectful – 'I won't test You' – but in reality, Ahaz is turning down God's invitation. He's missing an opportunity to see the Lord's saving power.

ASK

Are there areas of my life where I need the Lord's help but haven't invited it? What's stopping me? I bring them to God now in prayer.

— Selah

Who do I know who's struggling? Someone who feels attacked on all sides at present? I ask God to give them a sign of His hope and power.

— Selah

YIELD

As I return to the passage, I open my ears to hear Your Word at a deeper level, and my heart to yield to Your will once again.

'Again the LORD spoke to Ahaz, "Ask the LORD your God for a sign, whether in the deepest depths or in the highest heights." But Ahaz said, "I will not ask; I will not put the LORD to the test." Then Isaiah said, "Hear now, you house of David! Is it not enough to try the patience of humans? Will you try the patience of my God also? Therefore the Lord himself will give you a sign: the virgin will conceive and give birth to a son, and will call him Immanuel."' **Isaiah 7:10–14**

This sign, prophesied by Isaiah to Ahaz, points to the life of Mary, the mother of Jesus, centuries later. A miraculous pregnancy – a virgin birth – and a child with a hope-filled name: 'Immanuel', meaning, 'God with us'. The birth of Jesus kicks God's great salvation plan into high gear, and marks the moment when God enters His creation in a whole new way. Jesus, God in human skin, loved by a young mother, come to live with us.

Jesus, thank You for not abandoning me to the mess of my own making. Thank You for joining me in the muck and marvel of this life. I choose to keep You (not myself) at the front of my mind throughout this Christmas, and I choose to be ready to share with others the story of God with us.

Closing Prayer

Father, may I live this day, true to You, come what may.

Jesus, may I give this day, in kindness to all, in every way.

Spirit, may I love this day, proclaiming Christ in all I say.

Amen.

DAY 10

This week, in the season of Advent, we are exploring the journey of Jesus' mother Mary.

PAUSE

I pause now, breathe deeply, and re-centre my scattered senses on the presence of God.

— Selah

Lord, in this busy season, please help me to be still. I am opening my ears now to hear amazing things from You, quietly preparing my heart for the wonder of Your coming at Christmas.

REJOICE and REFLECT

What about God am I most grateful for today? I tell Him now.

Today we reflect on one of my heroes; the woman I always wanted (but never got) to play in my school nativity: Mary, the soon-to-be mother of Jesus. Luke introduces Mary as her life is about to be hijacked by God (with her permission!), so she can play a pivotal role in His redemption plan.

> 'In the sixth month of Elizabeth's pregnancy, God sent the angel
> Gabriel to Nazareth, a town in Galilee, to a virgin pledged to
> be married to a man named Joseph, a descendant of David.
> The virgin's name was Mary. The angel went to her and said,
> "Greetings, you who are highly favoured! The Lord is with you."
> Mary was greatly troubled at his words and wondered what kind
> of greeting this might be.' **Luke 1:26–29**

We tend to introduce ourselves differently, depending on who we're speaking to. Sometimes we might start talking about our families; other times it's our work, interests or where we're from. We generally choose the approach that forms the quickest bond.

Luke introduces Mary with where she lives, an indication of her age, her relationship status and name. But when the angel Gabriel greets her, he describes her very differently…

'Greetings, you who are highly favoured!'

ASK

For Gabriel, Mary's identity is rooted in what God thinks of her. What do I believe God thinks of me? I invite Him to tell me now…

— *Selah*

Who have I met or who will I meet today? What do I believe God thinks of them? I pray for each person now and listen for what God says about them.

— *Selah*

YIELD

As I return to the passage, I open my ears to hear Your Word at a deeper level, and my heart to yield to Your will once again.

'In the sixth month of Elizabeth's pregnancy, God sent the angel
Gabriel to Nazareth, a town in Galilee, to a virgin pledged to
be married to a man named Joseph, a descendant of David.
The virgin's name was Mary. The angel went to her and said,
"Greetings, you who are highly favoured! The Lord is with you."
Mary was greatly troubled at his words and wondered what kind
of greeting this might be.' **Luke 1:26–29**

With five words Mary's life changes forever: 'The Lord is with you.'
Before she hears or agrees to God's plan. Before she's pregnant. The
Lord is with her.

I find it mind-boggling that before I knew Jesus, before I understood
anything of His plans for my life, even before I said yes to following
Him, God knew who I was and He was with me.

God, I yield to this extraordinary truth that You are with me, whether
I'm conscious of it or not. Make me aware of Your presence now, and
through each hour of my day today.

Closing Prayer
Father, may I live this day, true to You, come what may.
Jesus, may I give this day, in kindness to all, in every way.
Spirit, may I love this day, proclaiming Christ in all I say.
Amen.

DAY 11

This week, in the season of Advent, we are exploring the journey of
Jesus' mother, Mary.

PAUSE
I pause now, breathe deeply, and re-centre my scattered senses on the
presence of God.

— Selah

Lord, in this busy season, please help me to be still. I am opening my ears now to hear amazing things from You, quietly preparing my heart for the wonder of Your coming at Christmas.

REJOICE and REFLECT

What about God am I most grateful for today? I tell Him now.

Today we reflect on young Mary, the soon-to-be mother of Jesus, coming face-to-face with the angel Gabriel. He has a message from God, just for her...

'But the angel said to her, "Do not be afraid, Mary, you have found favour with God. You will conceive and give birth to a son, and you are to call him Jesus. He will be great and will be called the Son of the Most High. The Lord God will give him the throne of his father David, and he will reign over Jacob's descendants for ever; his kingdom will never end."' **Luke 1:30–33**

In this situation, face-to-face with a messenger from God, abject fear seems like a totally understandable reaction. If I (Carla) were Mary, I would be freaking out that a) There's a real life angel; b) I've somehow caught the attention of the Almighty; c) Impossible things are about to happen and I'll be at the centre of them.

Gabriel is quick to reassure her: 'Do not be afraid, Mary, you have found favour with God.'

Fear can feel all-consuming. Maybe that's why 'Do not be afraid' is the most repeated command in Scripture. God's favour and love displace fear.

ASK

What frightens me at the moment? I ask God to put my fears into perspective and I welcome His love.

— Selah

Gabriel tells Mary God's purpose for her life. Who do I know who's feeling lost or looking for purpose? I pray for them now: Lord, guide them towards Your plan for their lives.

— Selah

YIELD

As I return to the passage, I open my ears to hear Your Word at a deeper level, and my heart to yield to Your will once again.

'But the angel said to her, "Do not be afraid, Mary, you have found favour with God. You will conceive and give birth to a son, and you are to call him Jesus. He will be great and will be called the Son of the Most High. The Lord God will give him the throne of his father David, and he will reign over Jacob's descendants for ever; his kingdom will never end."' **Luke 1:30–33**

This child will be the King that Israel has been waiting for, but His arrival is turning Mary's life upside down. She's engaged. Normally, next would come marriage, building a home, and then kids. Choosing to be part of God's plan will affect Mary's body, family, relationships, social status and probably more.

What areas of my life would I struggle to have turned upside down by God's plan?

— Selah

Jesus, I'm all Yours. Even the parts I find it hard to surrender. Holy Spirit, teach me to be like Mary, ready to trust the Lord and jump into His plans with everything I've got. God, use my body, my talents, my relationships, my income, all that You have given me, to expand Your kingdom.

Closing Prayer

Father, may I live this day, true to You, come what may.

Jesus, may I give this day, in kindness to all, in every way.

Spirit, may I love this day, proclaiming Christ in all I say.

Amen.

DAY 12

This week, in the season of Advent, we are exploring the journey of Jesus' mother, Mary.

PAUSE

I pause now, breathe deeply, and re-centre my scattered senses on the presence of God.

— Selah

Lord, in this busy season, please help me to be still. I am opening my ears now to hear amazing things from You, quietly preparing my heart for the wonder of Your coming at Christmas.

REJOICE and REFLECT

What about God am I most grateful for today? I tell Him now.

Today we're reflecting on the final part of Mary's encounter with the angel Gabriel. A conversation that will alter the course of her life forever. Mary has just heard that she will give birth to the Messiah, the Saviour Israel has been waiting for, and she responds with a question...

"'How will this be," Mary asked the angel, "since I am a virgin?" The angel answered, "The Holy Spirit will come on you, and the power of the Most High will overshadow you. So the holy one to be born will be called the Son of God. Even Elizabeth your relative is going to have a child in her old age, and she who was said to be unable to conceive is in her sixth month. For no word from God will ever fail." "I am the Lord's servant," Mary answered. "May your word to me be fulfilled." Then the angel left her.' **Luke 1:34–38**

Having heard about all God is planning through one, miraculous pregnancy, Mary has a refreshingly practical question. It's not, 'How is my kid going to become King?' It's not, 'How can someone rule forever?' Her question is something biological and logical: 'How can this happen? I'm a virgin!'

Gabriel's response? 'It's God's presence that will make God's plan a reality.'

ASK

If it's God's presence in my life that makes His plans a reality, are there any areas in which God feels absent or distant right now?

Lord, help me to know Your presence in the parts of my life that seem confusing, painful or even scary.

— Selah

Mary is standing on a cliff-edge, being asked to jump. Responding to God's invitation means risking rejection from her fiancé, Joseph, and all the challenge that came with being a single mum in that culture.

Lord, I pray for the single parents I know. Please give them strength and bless them with joy as they raise their children.

— Selah

YIELD

As I return to the passage, I open my ears to hear Your Word at a deeper level, and my heart to yield to Your will once again.

'"How will this be," Mary asked the angel, "since I am a virgin?"
The angel answered, "The Holy Spirit will come on you, and
the power of the Most High will overshadow you. So the holy
one to be born will be called the Son of God. Even Elizabeth
your relative is going to have a child in her old age, and she who
was said to be unable to conceive is in her sixth month. For no
word from God will ever fail." "I am the Lord's servant," Mary
answered. "May your word to me be fulfilled." Then the angel left
her.' **Luke 1:34–38**

'I am the Lord's servant.'

Mary is wholeheartedly on board with God's plan, even though it
will have far-reaching implications for her life. Her willing surrender
shows complete faith that God's Word can be depended on, and that
He's big enough to handle all the details.

*In what areas does it feel like God is asking me to take a leap of faith
right now?*

— Selah

*Lord, I am humbled by Mary's response. I think I trust You completely
until the moment You ask me to step out of my comfort zone. Use the
risk-taking moments in my life to teach me greater trust in Your Word
and care. I am Your servant, today and always.*

Closing Prayer

Father, may I live this day, true to You, come what may.
Jesus, may I give this day, in kindness to all, in every way.
Spirit, may I love this day, proclaiming Christ in all I say.
Amen.

DAY 13

This week, in the season of Advent, we are exploring the journey of Jesus' mother, Mary.

PAUSE

I pause now, breathe deeply, and re-centre my scattered senses on the presence of God.

— Selah

Lord, in this busy season, please help me to be still. I am opening my ears now to hear amazing things from You, quietly preparing my heart for the wonder of Your coming at Christmas.

REJOICE and REFLECT

What about God am I most grateful for today? I tell Him now.

Today we reflect on the first half of one of the most famous exclamations of praise in the Bible. Mary, who's now scandalously pregnant with the Son of God, is visiting her cousin Elizabeth. When Elizabeth and the baby in her womb realise the significance of Mary's pregnancy, praise flows from both cousins. Elizabeth says...

> "'Blessed is she who has believed that the Lord would fulfil his promises to her!"
> And Mary said:
> "My soul glorifies the Lord
> and my spirit rejoices in God my Saviour,
> for he has been mindful
> of the humble state of his servant.
> From now on all generations will call me blessed,
> for the Mighty One has done great things for me –
> holy is his name."' **Luke 1:45–49**

This must have been a time of great uncertainty for Mary as a young, unmarried mum-to-be. In her place, perhaps we'd be worried about our family's reaction to the news, nervous of each first encounter with relatives.

Elizabeth welcomes her – not with judgment or sorrow, but with joy for what God is up to. Imagine how Mary might feel in that moment.

ASK

Mary's praise bubbles up from deep within her – her soul and spirit. What's within my soul and spirit today?

— Selah

Together, Mary and Elizabeth overflow with gratitude and praise. Lord, would You stir the same grateful, worshipping spirit in my church. Make us a community, full of Your Holy Spirit, quick to praise You in all circumstances.

— Selah

YIELD

As I return to the passage, I open my ears to hear Your Word at a deeper level, and my heart to yield to Your will once again.

"'Blessed is she who has believed that the Lord would fulfil his
promises to her!"
And Mary said:
"My soul glorifies the Lord
 and my spirit rejoices in God my Saviour,
 for he has been mindful
 of the humble state of his servant.
 From now on all generations will call me blessed,
 for the Mighty One has done great things for me –
 holy is his name."' **Luke 1:45–49**

What great things has God done for Mary? Yes, she's pregnant with Jesus, but she doesn't sing, "'the Mighty One has done *a* great thing for me'. It's plural, not singular. She's praising Him for her child and much more.

> *Sometimes I find it easier to see the needs I'm facing than the blessings God has already given me. What great things has the Lord done for me?*
>
> — *Selah*
>
> *Lord, I confess I can be very ungrateful. I choose today to practise thanking You at every opportunity. Holy Spirit, make me aware of every good thing I encounter.*

Closing Prayer
Father, may I live this day, true to You, come what may.
Jesus, may I give this day, in kindness to all, in every way.
Spirit, may I love this day, proclaiming Christ in all I say.
Amen.

DAY 14

This week, in the season of Advent, we are exploring the journey of Jesus' mother, Mary.

PAUSE
> *I pause now, breathe deeply, and re-centre my scattered senses on the presence of God.*
>
> — *Selah*
>
> *Lord, in this busy season, please help me to be still. I am opening my ears now to hear amazing things from You, quietly preparing my heart for the wonder of Your coming at Christmas.*

REJOICE and REFLECT

What about God am I most grateful for today? I tell Him now.

Today we reflect on the second half of Mary's song of praise in Luke 1, often called the *Magnificat*. Her moving description of God has been read, meditated on, prayed and sung for centuries since. As you read her words now, invite the Holy Spirit to speak to you.

'His mercy extends to those who fear him,
from generation to generation.
He has performed mighty deeds with his arm;
he has scattered those who are proud in their inmost thoughts.
He has brought down rulers from their thrones
but has lifted up the humble.
He has filled the hungry with good things
but has sent the rich away empty.
He has helped his servant Israel,
remembering to be merciful
to Abraham and his descendants for ever,
just as he promised our ancestors.' **Luke 1:50–55**

Mary sings her song as a young, unmarried, pregnant woman, from an oppressed people. The themes she touches on – mercy, humility, satisfying the hungry – are like a foretaste of her Son's ministry.

Wow – these are potent words describing an active and powerful God who spans generations, favours the vulnerable and keeps His promises!

ASK

Mary's song describes the tenderness of God towards the vulnerable. Where do I feel vulnerable? I invite God into those parts of my life.

— Selah

Who needs the tenderness and protection of God right now? My elderly neighbour? The men and women who sleep rough on the streets of my city? The families quietly struggling with the financial burden of Christmas? God, I ask You for Your loving presence and intervention in their lives.

— *Selah*

YIELD

As I return to the passage, I open my ears to hear Your Word at a deeper level, and my heart to yield to Your will once again.

'His mercy extends to those who fear him,
from generation to generation.
He has performed mighty deeds with his arm;
he has scattered those who are proud in their inmost thoughts.
He has brought down rulers from their thrones
but has lifted up the humble.
He has filled the hungry with good things
but has sent the rich away empty.
He has helped his servant Israel,
remembering to be merciful
to Abraham and his descendants for ever,
just as he promised our ancestors.' **Luke 1:50–55**

What's striking about Mary's song is not its theology or eloquence, but its timing. Mary isn't singing this song at Jesus' birth. She's singing it while she's pregnant, while she's waiting. I wonder what role Mary's worship had in bringing God's plan to birth in her life?

What do I feel 'pregnant' with at the moment? What might come to birth if I worshipped like Mary?

— *Selah*

Lord, I choose to see Your goodness and greatness, even when my life feels neither good nor great. Help me to live this Advent worshipping You for what You've given me in Christ, and what You're yet to give me, and to the world, when He returns.

Closing Prayer

Father, may I live this day, true to You, come what may.
Jesus, may I give this day, in kindness to all, in every way.
Spirit, may I love this day, proclaiming Christ in all I say.
Amen.

DAY 15

Today is the third Sunday of Advent. As with the previous two Sundays, we'll be praying differently today from the rest of the week as we work through our Sabbath prayer...

As we journey towards Christmas, let us prepare our hearts for Christ's coming.

One of the earliest recorded prayers of the Church is the Aramaic word *maranatha*, which literally means, 'Come, Lord Jesus'. The Latin word *adventus* means the same thing – 'come'. This is a season of waiting and wanting; looking and longing; inviting Christ to come once more into our lives and into our world. Pause now and repeat this ancient prayer several times slowly:

Maranatha, come, Lord Jesus.

— *Selah*

We're going to stick with this simple prayer, *Maranatha*, a bit longer.

If you are aware of sinful thoughts, words or deeds in your life, acknowledge them now before the Lord, praying: *Maranatha, come, Lord Jesus.*

— *Selah*

Now think of someone who needs Christ's love today, praying for them: *Maranatha, come, Lord Jesus.*

— *Selah*

Next, remember your own local church and the many activities it has planned during this Christmas season, praying again: *Maranatha, come, Lord Jesus.*

— *Selah*

Finally, think of a place in the world that desperately needs Christ's comfort today, praying: *Maranatha, come, Lord Jesus.*

— *Selah*

In the twelfth century, Saint Bernard of Clairvaux, a forerunner of the Cistercian order of monks, notably said that Christ comes three times: in the past to Bethlehem at Christmas, in the future at the end of the age, and in the present day lives of believers. Let's pray for all three:

Thank You, Father, for loving us so much that You sent Your Son to save us.
Maranatha. May Jesus be born again among us this Christmas.
Thank You, Jesus, that You came before and You are coming again in glory.
Maranatha. We long for You to return and make all things new.
Thank You, Holy Spirit, for filling my life.
Maranatha. May the Lord Jesus Christ be born again in me today.

Blessing

May this day bring Sabbath rest to your heart and your home.

May your peace and perspective be renewed in the busyness of this season.

May your hand be free enough from spending and acquiring to receive God's gift.

May a little of the wonder of Christmas awaken the child within today.

May God's Word feed you and His Spirit lead you into the week and into the life to come.

WEEK THREE

Journeying with Joseph

PETE GREIG

DAY 16

It is the third week of Advent.

This week, since 1995, the world has marked South Africa's Day of Reconciliation, instigated by Nelson Mandela and Archbishop Desmond Tutu to commemorate the peaceful end to apartheid.

PAUSE

I pause now, breathe deeply, and re-centre my scattered senses on the presence of God.

— *Selah*

Father, as I spend time with You now, break my heart for the things that break Yours.
Jesus, show me how to act justly, love mercy and walk humbly with You today.
Holy Spirit, anoint me to proclaim good news to the poor. Amen.

REJOICE and REFLECT

What about God am I most grateful for today? I tell Him now.

Advent is an important time to be thinking about justice, mercy and reconciliation. As we do so today, our format is going to be a little different with a longer reading, not from the Bible. It comes from my book *How to Pray**, and reminds us of the extraordinary power of forgiveness and reconciliation.

Ruby Bridges was just six years old when she became the first African American to attend an all-white elementary school in New Orleans. Every day she was escorted by armed guards through angry crowds at the school gates. One woman screamed death threats at Ruby. Another protester held a black doll aloft in a coffin. Parents pulled their children out of the school. Having braved the crowd's hatred, Ruby would sit all alone in an empty classroom, wandering the corridors in break times, looking for other children. Images of this tiny little girl – so smartly dressed and clutching her school bag, guarded by Federal Marshalls twice her size – polarised America and the child psychologist Robert Coles offered Ruby counselling. Once a week he would sit in the humble home she shared with four siblings and her parents, who could neither read nor write. 'You looked like you were talking to the people in the street on your way into school yesterday,' he said on one occasion. 'Did you finally get angry with them? Were you telling them to leave you alone?'

'No, doctor,' replied Ruby politely. 'I didn't tell them anything. I didn't talk to them.'

'Well, who were you talking to?'

The little girl stared at him. 'I was talking to God. I was praying to God for the people in the street.'

'You were praying for them? But Ruby, why were you praying for them?'

Her eyes widened. 'Well, don't you think they need praying for?' Robert Coles was lost for words. Regaining his composure he whispered, 'What do you say when you pray for them, Ruby?'

'Oh, I always say the same thing. Please God, try to forgive these people because even if they say these mean things, they don't know what they're doing.'

ASK

Ruby was, of course, quoting the words of Jesus on the cross: 'Father, forgive them, for they do not know what they are doing' (Luke 23:34). She was resisting hatred with mercy; anger with amazing grace.

Is there anyone I know whose sins I am counting against them? What would it take for me to forgive them, to be reconciled with them, in this Christmas season?

— *Selah*

The apostle Paul says that God 'reconciled us to himself through Christ and gave us the ministry of reconciliation' (2 Cor. 5:18). Spend a little time now praying for reconciliation in a situation of discord – it might be a conflict in another land, or a very personal thing like a broken relationship in your own life. What might reconciliation actually look like in this situation? How might it come about? Pray that the Prince of Peace would rise with healing in His wings this Christmas. Pray against bitterness and fear. Pray: 'Father, forgive them, for they do not know what they are doing.'

And now I pray particularly for politicians working for peace and reconciliation in difficult areas of great conflict at this time of year.

YIELD

Take a moment to listen to or sing the song *Amazing Grace* and reflect on its words.

Closing Prayer

Father, may I live this day, true to You, come what may.
Jesus, may I give this day, in kindness to all, in every way.
Spirit, may I love this day, proclaiming Christ in all I say.
Amen.

*Pete Greig, *How to Pray* (London: Hodder & Stoughton, 2019)

DAY 17

It is the third week of Advent.

PAUSE

I pause now, breathe deeply, and re-centre my scattered senses on the presence of God.

— Selah

Lord, in this busy season, please help me to be still. I am opening my ears now to hear amazing things from You, quietly preparing my heart for the wonder of Your coming at Christmas.

REJOICE and REFLECT

What about God am I most grateful for today? I tell Him now.

For most of the rest of this week we're going to be tracing Joseph's journey to Bethlehem, trying to see the old, familiar Christmas story through his unique perspective.

'This is how the birth of Jesus the Messiah came about: his mother Mary was pledged to be married to Joseph, but before they came together, she was found to be pregnant through the Holy Spirit. Because Joseph her husband was faithful to the law, and yet did not want to expose her to public disgrace, he had in mind to divorce her quietly.

But after he had considered this, an angel of the Lord appeared to him in a dream and said, "Joseph son of David, do not be afraid to take Mary home as your wife, because what is conceived in her is from the Holy Spirit. She will give birth to a son, and you are to give him the name Jesus, because he will save his people from their sins." When Joseph woke up, he did what the angel of the Lord had commanded him and took Mary home as his wife. But he did not consummate their marriage until she gave birth to a son. And he gave him the name Jesus.' **Matthew 1:18–21, 24–25**

Joseph has a uniquely lonely calling. Try to imagine him waking up from that dream. God has said that Mary's pregnancy is indeed miraculous and that he should go ahead and marry her. Is he awestruck or sceptical? Relieved or terrified? Questioning or convinced?

Joseph could easily have felt deeply indignant and insecure. I wonder if he felt like a bit of a fool, deprived of true fatherhood, bypassed and sidelined.

ASK

How do I tend to respond when God shows me something I find hard to believe or receive? Do I feel bypassed or sidelined in different areas of my life? I talk to God now.

— Selah

I think of parents I know in complex family situations. I pray now for clarity in the midst of confusion, comfort in the place of disappointment and guidance when they don't know what to do.

— Selah

YIELD

As I return to the passage, I open my ears to hear Your Word at a deeper level, and my heart to yield to Your will once again.

'This is how the birth of Jesus the Messiah came about: his mother Mary was pledged to be married to Joseph, but before they came together, she was found to be pregnant through the Holy Spirit. Because Joseph her husband was faithful to the law, and yet did not want to expose her to public disgrace, he had in mind to divorce her quietly.

But after he had considered this, an angel of the Lord appeared to him in a dream and said, "Joseph son of David, do not be afraid to take Mary home as your wife, because what is conceived in her is from the Holy Spirit. She will give birth to a son, and you are to give him the name Jesus, because he will save his people from their sins."

When Joseph woke up, he did what the angel of the Lord had commanded him and took Mary home as his wife. But he did not consummate their marriage until she gave birth to a son. And he gave him the name Jesus.' **Matthew 1:18–21,24–25**

Joseph intended to divorce Mary because that was what the law required, but he planned to do so quietly without exposing her to public disgrace. He was principled – a man of integrity who knew that 'the right thing to do is always the right thing to do' – but he was also kind and compassionate.

Sometimes we can be too principled at the expense of kindness, or we can be too 'kind' at the expense of biblical integrity.

Lord, search me and show me my motivations. Bring to mind the places I need to choose kindness, and situations where I need to make brave choices. Like Joseph, help me to hear Your commands to me today and obey them. Lord, I yield to You.

Closing Prayer

Father, may I live this day, true to You, come what may.
Jesus, may I give this day, in kindness to all, in every way.
Spirit, may I love this day, proclaiming Christ in all I say.
Amen.

DAY 18

It is the third week of Advent.

PAUSE

I pause now, breathe deeply, and re-centre my scattered senses on the presence of God.

— Selah

Lord, in this busy season, please help me to be still. I am opening my ears now to hear amazing things from You, quietly preparing my heart for the wonder of Your coming at Christmas.

REJOICE and REFLECT

What about God am I most grateful for today? I tell Him now.

This week, we continue to trace Joseph's journey to Bethlehem, by returning to yesterday's passage in Matthew 1:

> 'This is how the birth of Jesus the Messiah came about: his mother Mary was pledged to be married to Joseph, but before they came together, she was found to be pregnant through the Holy Spirit. Because Joseph her husband was faithful to the law, and yet did not want to expose her to public disgrace, he had in mind to divorce her quietly.
> But after he had considered this, an angel of the Lord appeared to him in a dream and said, "Joseph son of David, do not be afraid to take Mary home as your wife, because what is conceived in her is from the Holy Spirit. She will give birth to a son, and you are to give him the name Jesus, because he will save his people from their sins."
> When Joseph woke up, he did what the angel of the Lord had commanded him and took Mary home as his wife. But he did not consummate their marriage until she gave birth to a son. And he gave him the name Jesus.' **Matthew 1:18–21,24–25**

It's interesting to note how often God speaks to Joseph through angelic dreams, particularly as his namesake in the Old Testament was also a dreamer. Joseph is encouraged to marry Mary by an angel in a dream. Later, he's warned to flee with his family to Egypt by an angel in a dream, and then he's given the all-clear to return home – once again, by an angel in a dream. This seems to have been the primary way in which God led Joseph.

ASK

How does God normally speak to me? Through Scripture? Pictures? Other people? Or dreams, like Joseph?

When did God last speak to me clearly? Have I completely obeyed?

— Selah

Where are the situations of danger in our world today? God, I pray that You would speak to those at risk, like You did to Joseph, that You would intervene and lead people to safety.

— Selah

YIELD

As I return to the passage, I open my ears to hear Your Word at a deeper level, and my heart to yield to Your will once again.

'This is how the birth of Jesus the Messiah came about: his mother Mary was pledged to be married to Joseph, but before they came together, she was found to be pregnant through the Holy Spirit. Because Joseph her husband was faithful to the law, and yet did not want to expose her to public disgrace, he had in mind to divorce her quietly.

But after he had considered this, an angel of the Lord appeared to him in a dream and said, "Joseph son of David, do not be afraid to take Mary home as your wife, because what is conceived in her is from the Holy Spirit. She will give birth to a son, and you are to give him the name Jesus, because he will save his people from their sins." When Joseph woke up, he did what the angel of the Lord had commanded him and took Mary home as his wife. But he did not consummate their marriage until she gave birth to a son. And he gave him the name Jesus.' **Matthew 1:18–21,24–25**

Joseph was possibly the third person to have an angel visit him in the build up to Jesus' birth, and he wouldn't be the last.

It was Charles Wesley, born 18 December 1707, who wrote the famous carol *Hark! The Herald Angels Sing*. This time next week, billions of people around the world will be celebrating the one 'born to raise the sons of earth, born to give them second birth'.

Jesus, I yield to You, the King of kings, heralded by angels.
I pray now for my friends and family who don't yet know You, the
new-born King, that they might encounter You this Christmas, and
yield to You too.

Closing Prayer

Father, may I live this day, true to You, come what may.
Jesus, may I give this day, in kindness to all, in every way.
Spirit, may I love this day, proclaiming Christ in all I say.
Amen.

DAY 19

It is the third week of Advent.

PAUSE

I pause now, breathe deeply, and re-centre my scattered senses on the
presence of God.

— Selah

Lord, in this busy season, please help me to be still. I am opening my
ears now to hear amazing things from You, quietly preparing my heart
for the wonder of Your coming at Christmas.

REJOICE and REFLECT

What about God am I most grateful for today? I tell Him now.

Today, we're doing something unusual. We are returning for a third time
to the passage about Joseph in Matthew 1. As we continue to trace Joseph's
journey, Holy Spirit, would You bring new depths of understanding.

'This is how the birth of Jesus the Messiah came about: his mother Mary was pledged to be married to Joseph, but before they came together, she was found to be pregnant through the Holy Spirit. Because Joseph her husband was faithful to the law, and yet did not want to expose her to public disgrace, he had in mind to divorce her quietly.

But after he had considered this, an angel of the Lord appeared to him in a dream and said, "Joseph son of David, do not be afraid to take Mary home as your wife, because what is conceived in her is from the Holy Spirit. She will give birth to a son, and you are to give him the name Jesus, because he will save his people from their sins."

When Joseph woke up, he did what the angel of the Lord had commanded him and took Mary home as his wife. But he did not consummate their marriage until she gave birth to a son. And he gave him the name Jesus.' **Matthew 1:18–21,24–25**

We don't know much about Joseph. He's only mentioned a handful of times in the Gospels. We do know that he was a working man – a carpenter. In many ways, he was called to play second fiddle to his wife and stepson. That's not an easy thing to do.

ASK

I ask You, Father, for Joseph's humility and grace. Everyone seems to want to be a 'somebody' in this world, but if You're calling me to be a 'nobody', help me to stop competing and comparing myself with others, and to start preferring and promoting them instead.

— Selah

I ask You, Lord, to show me someone this week who feels lonely, scared, forgotten or bypassed this Christmas. Help me to show them Your love in a practical, personal way.

— Selah

YIELD

As I return to the passage, I open my ears to hear Your Word at a deeper level, and my heart to yield to Your will once again.

'This is how the birth of Jesus the Messiah came about: his mother Mary was pledged to be married to Joseph, but before they came together, she was found to be pregnant through the Holy Spirit. Because Joseph her husband was faithful to the law, and yet did not want to expose her to public disgrace, he had in mind to divorce her quietly.

But after he had considered this, an angel of the Lord appeared to him in a dream and said, "Joseph son of David, do not be afraid to take Mary home as your wife, because what is conceived in her is from the Holy Spirit. She will give birth to a son, and you are to give him the name Jesus, because he will save his people from their sins." When Joseph woke up, he did what the angel of the Lord had commanded him and took Mary home as his wife. But he did not consummate their marriage until she gave birth to a son. And he gave him the name Jesus.' **Matthew 1:18–21,24–25**

Over the last three days we have focused a lot on the price of Joseph's calling, but it was also an extraordinary privilege. Joseph was trusted to be a parent to the Son of God. That's a mind-blowing responsibility. He was also told to name the one whose name is above every other. The price of obedience is always outweighed by the privilege of the call. As Joseph's son James, the half-brother of Jesus, writes: 'Humble yourselves before the Lord, and he will lift you up' (James 4:10).

Make *The Message* paraphrase of Romans 12:9–10 your prayer today:

Lord, help me love from the centre of who I am; I don't want to fake it. I run for dear life from evil; I hold on for dear life to good. Help me to be a good friend who loves deeply; help me to practice playing second fiddle.

Closing Prayer

Father, may I live this day, true to You, come what may.

Jesus, may I give this day, in kindness to all, in every way.

Spirit, may I love this day, proclaiming Christ in all I say.

Amen.

DAY 20

It is the third week of advent.

PAUSE

I pause now, breathe deeply, and re-centre my scattered senses on the presence of God.

— Selah

Lord, in this busy season, please help me to be still. I am opening my ears now to hear amazing things from You, quietly preparing my heart for the wonder of Your coming at Christmas.

REJOICE and REFLECT

What about God am I most grateful for today? I tell Him now.

Today, we look at a particular moment in Joseph's story from Luke's perspective. In this passage we glimpse the wider political and national landscape Jesus was born into...

'In those days Caesar Augustus issued a decree that a census should be taken of the entire Roman world. (This was the first census that took place while Quirinius was governor of Syria.) And everyone went to their own town to register. So Joseph also went up from the town of Nazareth in Galilee to Judea, to Bethlehem the town of David, because he belonged to the house and line of David. He went there to register with Mary, who

was pledged to be married to him and was expecting a child.'
Luke 2:1–5

ASK

Jesus was born in the royal city of Bethlehem because Joseph belonged to the house of David. Isn't it interesting how God works through family trees? At Christmas we enjoy the blessing and endure the brokenness of families. Joseph's genealogy traces right back to Bathsheba, with whom King David had an adulterous and murderous affair.

How am I feeling about the people I'll be seeing next week for Christmas? Lord Jesus, thank You for the blessing of those in my family who have loved me most. Thank You that You can also bring blessing through the broken parts of my family history. This Christmas I ask You to give me extra helpings of patience to be kind to difficult relatives. I take time now to name those for whom I'm especially grateful or especially concerned.

— Selah

I ask You, Father, to save entire families this Christmas. I pray for those who are trapped in generational cycles of brokenness, poverty, addiction and abuse.
Change family trees.
Break vicious cycles.
Convert curses to blessings in the name of Jesus Christ, my Saviour, Son of David... and of Bathsheba too.

— Selah

YIELD

As I return to the passage, I open my ears to hear Your Word at a deeper level, and my heart to yield to Your will once again.

'In those days Caesar Augustus issued a decree that a census should be taken of the entire Roman world. (This was the first census that took place while Quirinius was governor of Syria.) And everyone went to their own town to register. So Joseph also went up from the town of Nazareth in Galilee to Judea, to Bethlehem the town of David, because he belonged to the house and line of David. He went there to register with Mary, who was pledged to be married to him and was expecting a child.'
Luke 2:1–5

God works through families, but also through the actions of difficult politicians like Caesar Augustus and Quirinius, to establish His own government of peace.

— Selah

Lord, I ask You to work in my life this Christmas – through even the unlikeliest family members and the most challenging leaders. I accept and bless the family You have given me, and the government You have put in power over me – for now!

Closing Prayer

Father, may I live this day, true to You, come what may.
Jesus, may I give this day, in kindness to all, in every way.
Spirit, may I love this day, proclaiming Christ in all I say.
Amen.

DAY 21

It is the third week of advent.

PAUSE

I pause now, breathe deeply, and re-centre my scattered senses on the presence of God.

— Selah

Lord, in this busy season, please help me to be still. I am opening my ears now to hear amazing things from You, quietly preparing my heart for the wonder of Your coming at Christmas.

REJOICE and REFLECT

What about God am I most grateful for today? I tell Him now.

Today we conclude our reflections on Joseph's journey to Bethlehem, which leads up to the birth of Jesus.

'Joseph also went up from Galilee, from the city of Nazareth, to Judea, to the city of David which is called Bethlehem, because he was of the house and family of David, in order to register along with Mary, who was engaged to him, and was with child. While they were there, the days were completed for her to give birth. And she gave birth to her firstborn son; and she wrapped Him in cloths, and laid Him in a manger, because there was no room for them in the inn.' **Luke 2:4–7 (NASB)**

That innkeeper missed the biggest opportunity of his life when he forced a heavily pregnant woman to sleep in his barn instead of finding her a room. In hindsight, it was a pretty epic fail. He could have kicked out someone less deserving, or even given up his own bedroom for Mary and Joseph for a night. In later years, when Jesus' fame began to spread, he must have regretted it deeply. He could so easily have been a hero in this story, but because he was driven by protocol and profit, or simply stressed and busy, he missed out.

ASK

I ask You, Lord, to help me to be sacrificially and imaginatively hospitable this Christmas, not just in my home, but in my heart and my busy schedule. Help me, as I think now about the people

I'll be spending Christmas with, to receive unexpected pressures as opportunities to host You, to go the extra mile and to be kind.

— Selah

I ask You, Father, to bless those who feel unwelcome in our society this Christmas: refugees, those who are homeless and those who are in prison. Give grace and joy to those who are ministering to them, and move by Your Spirit to show them that the nativity story belongs to them too. Show me if there are particular people for whom You want me to pray now.

— Selah

YIELD

As I return to the passage, I open my ears to hear Your Word at a deeper level, and my heart to yield to Your will once again.

'Joseph also went up from Galilee, from the city of Nazareth, to Judea, to the city of David which is called Bethlehem, because he was of the house and family of David, in order to register along with Mary, who was engaged to him, and was with child. While they were there, the days were completed for her to give birth. And she gave birth to her firstborn son; and she wrapped Him in cloths, and laid Him in a manger, because there was no room for them in the inn.' **Luke 2:4–7 (NASB)**

I wonder how Joseph felt. How terrible to have your wife give birth in a barn! In not finding somewhere safe and warm for Mary, I wonder if he felt like he failed to be a good husband, and maybe even failed God, who had charged him with the mighty responsibility of raising this child.

— Selah

Lord, I yield my sense of inadequacy and failure to Your bigger, more beautiful plan. Please make 'all things work together for good' this Christmas, in me and, if necessary, in spite of me.

Closing Prayer

Father, may I live this day, true to You, come what may.
Jesus, may I give this day, in kindness to all, in every way.
Spirit, may I love this day, proclaiming Christ in all I say.
Amen.

DAY 22

Today is the fourth Sunday of Advent. We return, for the last time before Christmas Day, to our Sabbath prayer...

> *As we journey towards Christmas, let us prepare our hearts for Christ's coming.*

One of the earliest recorded prayers of the Church is the Aramaic word *maranatha*, which literally means, 'Come, Lord Jesus'. The Latin word *adventus* means the same thing – 'come'. This is a season of waiting and wanting; looking and longing; inviting Christ to come once more into our lives and into our world. Pause now and repeat this ancient prayer several times slowly:

> *Maranatha, come, Lord Jesus.*

> *— Selah*

We're going to stick with this simple prayer, *Maranatha*, a bit longer.

If you are aware of sinful thoughts, words or deeds in your life, acknowledge them now before the Lord, praying: *Maranatha, come, Lord Jesus.*

— Selah

Now think of someone who needs Christ's love today, praying for them: *Maranatha, come, Lord Jesus.*

— Selah

Next, remember your own local church and the many activities it has planned during this Christmas season, praying again: *Maranatha, come, Lord Jesus.*

— Selah

Finally, think of a place in the world that desperately needs Christ's comfort today, praying: *Maranatha, come, Lord Jesus.*

— Selah

In the twelfth century, Saint Bernard of Clairvaux, a forerunner of the Cistercian order of monks, notably said that Christ comes three times: in the past to Bethlehem at Christmas, in the future at the end of the age, and in the present day lives of believers. Let's pray for all three:

> *Thank You, Father, for loving us so much that You sent Your Son*
> *to save us.*
> *Maranatha. May Jesus be born again among us this Christmas.*
> *Thank You, Jesus, that You came before and You are coming*
> *again in glory.*
> *Maranatha. We long for You to return and make all things new.*
> *Thank You, Holy Spirit, for filling my life.*
> *Maranatha. May the Lord Jesus Christ be born again in me today.*

Blessing

May this day bring Sabbath rest to your heart and your home.

May your peace and perspective be renewed in the busyness of this season.

May your hand be free enough from spending and acquiring to receive God's gift.

May a little of the wonder of Christmas awaken the child within today.

May God's Word feed you and His Spirit lead you into the week and into the life to come.

WEEK FOUR

Journeying to Jesus

PHIL TOGWELL

DAY 23

This week is the fourth week of Advent.

PAUSE

I pause now, breathe deeply, and re-centre my scattered senses on the presence of God.

— Selah

Lord, in this busy season, please help me to be still. I am opening my ears now to hear amazing things from You, quietly preparing my heart for the wonder of Your coming at Christmas.

REJOICE and REFLECT

What about God am I most grateful for today? I tell Him now.

This week we're reflecting on the drama of Jesus' birth. We'll join the first of the main characters tomorrow, but today, we'll begin with a prophecy found in Isaiah 9, written over 700 years before Jesus was born.

> 'For to us a child is born,
> to us a son is given,
> and the government will be on his shoulders.
> And he will be called
> Wonderful Counsellor, Mighty God,
> Everlasting Father, Prince of Peace.
> Of the greatness of his government and peace
> there will be no end.
> He will reign on David's throne
> and over his kingdom,
> establishing and upholding it
> with justice and righteousness
> from that time on and for ever.

The zeal of the LORD Almighty
will accomplish this.' **Isaiah 9:6–7**

Christmas can be a frenzy of activity. Decorations are displayed. Presents are bought, wrapped and exchanged. Food is planned and prepared... and eaten! Friends and relatives come and go... or we go to them, and come back again. And then a few days later, sometime after Christmas Day, the decorations go back in their boxes and it's all over for another year.

So much of what Christmas has come to mean is temporary. And yet Isaiah describes something very different, something everlasting. Isaiah foresaw someone who would change everything: Jesus, the forever King.

ASK

As I think about Isaiah's words, I still myself for a moment. I try to imagine eternity, and I ask myself, how does it feel to know that I will live forever?

— Selah

I ask You, Everlasting Father, to make me more aware that the choices I make, the way I speak and the prayers I pray for people, echo for eternity. Who have I met, or will I meet, today? I pray my very best prayer for them now.

— Selah

YIELD

As I return to the passage, I open my ears to hear Your Word at a deeper level, and my heart to yield to Your will once again.

'For to us a child is born,
to us a son is given,
and the government will be on his shoulders.
And he will be called

Wonderful Counsellor, Mighty God,
Everlasting Father, Prince of Peace.
Of the greatness of his government and peace
there will be no end.
He will reign on David's throne
and over his kingdom,
establishing and upholding it
with justice and righteousness
from that time on and for ever.
The zeal of the LORD Almighty
will accomplish this.' **Isaiah 9:6–7**

*Who do I need Jesus to be today? Wonderful Counsellor? Mighty God?
Everlasting Father? Prince of Peace?*

— Selah

*I yield to You, Wonderful Counsellor. I will trust You when I feel
broken. I yield to You, Mighty God. I will trust You when I am afraid.
I yield to You, Everlasting Father. I will trust You when I am alone.
I yield to You, Prince of Peace. I will trust You when the storms
are raging.*

Closing Prayer

Father, may I live this day, true to You, come what may.
Jesus, may I give this day, in kindness to all, in every way.
Spirit, may I love this day, proclaiming Christ in all I say.
Amen.

DAY 24

It is the fourth week of Advent.

PAUSE

I pause now, breathe deeply, and re-centre my scattered senses on the presence of God.

— Selah

Lord, in this busy season, please help me to be still. I am opening my ears now to hear amazing things from You, quietly preparing my heart for the wonder of Your coming at Christmas.

REJOICE and REFLECT

What about God am I most grateful for today? I tell Him now.

Today, we're reflecting on the second chapter of Luke's Gospel, where we meet the first of the characters who participate in the drama of Jesus' birth: the shepherds.

'And there were shepherds living out in the fields near by, keeping watch over their flocks at night. An angel of the Lord appeared to them, and the glory of the Lord shone around them, and they were terrified. But the angel said to them, "Do not be afraid. I bring you good news that will cause great joy for all the people."' **Luke 2:8–10**

Imagine the scene. The shepherds were just doing what shepherds do – watching their sheep – when the angels appeared. An ordinary day suddenly became extraordinary... not to mention terrifying!

We see this pattern throughout the Bible. God interrupts people while they are going about ordinary tasks. Matthew was in his tax-collecting booth when Jesus passed by and told him to leave everything behind and follow Him. The boy Samuel was asleep when

God spoke, audibly, in his room. And Moses was also watching his sheep when a strange burning bush caught his attention.

ASK

As I think about the way that the shepherds responded to the angel's announcement, I ask myself, how interruptible am I? Amidst the busyness of Christmas, how can I be more open to the unexpected? I ask You, God, to speak to me when and where I least expect it.

— Selah

I ask You, God, to speak to my friends, my family, to those I know who need to hear 'good news that will bring great joy'. As I think of three people in particular right now, I ask You, God, to interrupt them with the good news of Jesus this Christmas.

— Selah

YIELD

As I return to the passage, I open my ears to hear Your Word at a deeper level, and my heart to yield to Your will once again.

'And there were shepherds living out in the fields near by, keeping watch over their flocks at night. An angel of the Lord appeared to them, and the glory of the Lord shone around them, and they were terrified. But the angel said to them, "Do not be afraid. I bring you good news that will cause great joy for all the people."' **Luke 2:8–10**

The shepherds were terrified as the angel announced the birth of Jesus, but their fear quickly turned to 'great joy' when they went to see Him for themselves. A little later in this chapter, Luke writes that 'the shepherds returned, glorifying and praising God for all the things they had seen and heard'. The good news became great joy for them, and for 'all the people' who heard them.

I confess that I am fearful and anxious about lots of things – some big things, and some so small that I am embarrassed to admit them. But they rob me of 'great joy'. I yield all of my fears and anxieties to You, God. I choose to trust You... and I make room for 'great joy'!

Closing Prayer

Father, may I live this day, true to You, come what may.
Jesus, may I give this day, in kindness to all, in every way.
Spirit, may I love this day, proclaiming Christ in all I say.
Amen.

DAY 25

It is the fourth week of Advent.

PAUSE

I pause now, breathe deeply, and re-centre my scattered senses on the presence of God.

— Selah

Lord, in this busy season, please help me to be still. I am opening my ears now to hear amazing things from You, quietly preparing my heart for the wonder of Your coming at Christmas.

REJOICE and REFLECT

What about God am I most grateful for today? I tell Him now.

Today we're reflecting on Luke 2, which begins with the angel of the Lord appearing to the shepherds and announcing the birth of Jesus.

"'Today in the town of David a Saviour has been born to you; he is the Messiah, the Lord. This will be a sign to you: you will find a baby wrapped in cloths and lying in a manger." Suddenly a great company

of the heavenly host appeared with the angel, praising God and saying, "Glory to God in the highest heaven, and on earth peace to those on whom his favour rests."' **Luke 2:11–14**

The last books of the Old Testament were written around 400 years before the first books of the New Testament. The silence of those 400 years comes to an end in a spectacular way – with a baby born to a teenage mother, surrounded by hosts of angels all singing, 'Glory to God in the highest heaven, and on earth peace to those on whom his favour rests.'

Those angels got the party started!

ASK

As I pause for a few moments, I ask myself, in what ways have I experienced the peace and presence of God this year? I give glory to God for them.

— Selah

Who do I know that needs to experience the peace and presence of God today? As I think of people I know who are suffering; those who are lonely this Christmas; those who are finding life difficult for whatever reason; I ask You, God, to bring peace to them.

— Selah

YIELD

As I return to the passage, I open my ears to hear Your Word at a deeper level, and my heart to yield to Your will once again.

"'Today in the town of David a Saviour has been born to you; he is the Messiah, the Lord. This will be a sign to you: You will find a baby wrapped in cloths and lying in a manger." Suddenly a great company of the heavenly host appeared with the angel, praising God and saying, "Glory to God in the highest heaven, and on earth peace to those on whom his favour rests."' **Luke 2:11–14**

It's easy to forget that the events surrounding Jesus' birth weren't as pretty as the Christmas cards on our shelves. Mary, Joseph and their son were refugees, about to leave home and travel hundreds of miles to flee persecution, fearing for their lives. This is the world that Jesus was born into, and sadly, this is the world that many are born into today. Today's world needs peace. Today's world needs the Prince of Peace.

John famously wrote that it was because God loved the whole world that He sent His only Son, Jesus, to be born, to live, to die and to rise again. And God did it because the world needs peace.

God, today I yield to Your peace-plan for my life. Help me to seek first the kingdom of peace in the world, to be a peacemaker in a divided world.

Closing Prayer
Father, may I live this day, true to You, come what may.
Jesus, may I give this day, in kindness to all, in every way.
Spirit, may I love this day, proclaiming Christ in all I say.
Amen.

DAY 26

It is the fourth week of Advent.

PAUSE

I pause now, breathe deeply, and re-centre my scattered senses on the presence of God.

— Selah

Lord, in this busy season, please help me to be still. I am opening my ears now to hear amazing things from You, quietly preparing my heart for the wonder of meeting with You.

REJOICE and REFLECT

What about God am I most grateful for today? I tell Him now.

Today we're reflecting on chapter two of Matthew's Gospel, where we join the Magi, or 'the wise men' as they are more commonly known, on their journey to find Jesus.

> 'After Jesus was born in Bethlehem in Judea, during the time of King Herod, Magi from the east came to Jerusalem and asked, "Where is the one who has been born king of the Jews? We saw his star when it rose and have come to worship him."... the star they had seen when it rose went ahead of them until it stopped over the place where the child was... On coming to the house, they saw the child with his mother Mary, and they bowed down and worshipped him. Then they opened their treasures and presented him with gifts of gold, frankincense and myrrh.' **Matthew 2:1–2,9,11**

There's a lot that we don't know about the men who followed the star to find Jesus. Who were they? Were they wise men or kings or astrologers? Where did they come from? And how many of them were there? Tradition says there were three, but the Bible doesn't actually tell us. Luke simply writes that 'Magi from the east came to Jerusalem', and they came looking for Jesus.

ASK

My life can be complicated, and I have lots of questions about lots of things, but I put all of that aside for a moment and I ask myself an important question: what am I looking for? What am I searching for? I ask You, God, to guide me on my journey.

— Selah

The Magi came looking for Jesus. Who do I know is looking for Jesus, even though they might not realise it yet? I ask You, Jesus, to help them find You.

— Selah

YIELD

As I return to the passage, I open my ears to hear Your Word at a deeper level, and my heart to yield to Your will once again.

'After Jesus was born in Bethlehem in Judea, during the time of King Herod, Magi from the east came to Jerusalem and asked, "Where is the one who has been born king of the Jews? We saw his star when it rose and have come to worship him."... the star they had seen when it rose went ahead of them until it stopped over the place where the child was... On coming to the house, they saw the child with his mother Mary, and they bowed down and worshipped him. Then they opened their treasures and presented him with gifts of gold, frankincense and myrrh.'
Matthew 2:1–2,9,11

The famous carol *In the Bleak Midwinter* is based on a poem by Christina Rossetti, and it includes a verse about the gifts that the shepherds and the Magi gave to Jesus:

'What can I give Him, poor as I am?
If I were a shepherd, I would bring a lamb;
If I were a wise man, I would do my part;
Yet what I can I give Him: give my heart.'

Jesus, I give You my heart, my hopes and my desires.
I also give You my mind, my thoughts and my ideas.
I give You my strength, my body and my energy.
And I give You my soul, the deepest part of who I am.
I yield all that I am to You today.

Closing Prayer

Father, may I live this day, true to You, come what may.

Jesus, may I give this day, in kindness to all, in every way.

Spirit, may I love this day, proclaiming Christ in all I say.

Amen.

DAY 27

This is the fourth week of Advent.

PAUSE

I pause now, breathe deeply, and re-centre my scattered senses on the presence of God.

— Selah

Lord, in this busy season, please help me to be still. I am opening my ears now to hear amazing things from You, quietly preparing my heart for the wonder of meeting with You.

REJOICE and REFLECT

What about God am I most grateful for today? I tell Him now.

Today we continue reflect on chapter two of Luke's Gospel, where we meet Simeon, who had been waiting patiently for God to fulfill a promise.

'Now there was a man in Jerusalem called Simeon, who was righteous and devout. He was waiting for the consolation of Israel, and the Holy Spirit was on him. It had been revealed to him by the Holy Spirit that he would not die before he had seen the Lord's Messiah. Moved by the Spirit, he went into the temple courts. When the parents brought in the child Jesus to do for him what the custom of the Law required, Simeon took him in his

arms and praised God, saying:
"Sovereign Lord, as you have promised,
you now dismiss your servant in peace.
For my eyes have seen your salvation,
which you have prepared in the sight of all nations:
a light for revelation to the Gentiles,
and the glory of your people Israel.'" **Luke 2:25–32**

Waiting for something that we want is never easy. In his letter to the church in Galatia, the apostle Paul describes patience as a fruit of the Spirit. Like a fruit, patience grows over time, in season and out of season.

Although every painting of this passage depicts Simeon as an old man, Luke doesn't actually tell us whether he was old or not. Simeon may have been waiting for a short time, or for many years. All we know is that he was full of the Holy Spirit, and that he was prepared to wait.

ASK

I ask myself, what am I waiting for at the moment? What am I hoping for and dreaming about? Help me, God, to become more patient, to trust that You are with me – in season and out of season.

— Selah

As I bring to mind those I know whose dreams have not come to pass; those who are finding it difficult to hope; those who need consolation: I ask You, God, to be with them today.

— Selah

YIELD

As I return to the passage, I open my ears to hear Your Word at a deeper level, and my heart to yield to Your will once again.

'Now there was a man in Jerusalem called Simeon, who was righteous and devout. He was waiting for the consolation of

Israel, and the Holy Spirit was on him. It had been revealed to him by the Holy Spirit that he would not die before he had seen the Lord's Messiah. Moved by the Spirit, he went into the temple courts. When the parents brought in the child Jesus to do for him what the custom of the Law required, Simeon took him in his arms and praised God, saying:
"Sovereign Lord, as you have promised,
you now dismiss your servant in peace.
For my eyes have seen your salvation,
which you have prepared in the sight of all nations:
a light for revelation to the Gentiles,
and the glory of your people Israel."' **Luke 2:25–32**

Luke says that the Holy Spirit was 'on' Simeon. Then Luke says that the Holy Spirit had promised Simeon that he would see the Lord's Messiah before he died, and that Simeon was fully and faithfully focused on the fulfilment of that promise. Finally, Luke says that when Simeon was 'moved by the Holy Spirit', he went straight to the temple courts where he met Jesus.

How have I been aware of the Holy Spirit over the last few days?

— Selah

Holy Spirit, I yield to You. Help me to be more sensitive to You. Move me today, in whatever ways You need to, and bring me to Jesus.

Closing Prayer
Father, may I live this day, true to You, come what may.
Jesus, may I give this day, in kindness to all, in every way.
Spirit, may I love this day, proclaiming Christ in all I say.
Amen.

DAY 28

This is the fourth week of Advent.

PAUSE

I pause now, breathe deeply, and re-centre my scattered senses on the presence of God.

— Selah

Lord, in this busy season, please help me to be still. I am opening my ears now to hear amazing things from You, quietly preparing my heart for the wonder of meeting with You.

REJOICE and REFLECT

What about God am I most grateful for today? I tell Him now.

Today is our last day reflecting on chapter two of Luke's Gospel. Throughout this week we've been meeting some of the characters who participated in the drama of Jesus' birth, and today we finish with Anna as she joins Mary, Joseph, Jesus and Simeon in the temple.

'There was also a prophet, Anna, the daughter of Penuel, of the tribe of Asher. She was very old; she had lived with her husband seven years after her marriage, and then she was a widow until she was eighty-four. She never left the temple but worshipped night and day, fasting and praying. Coming up to them at that very moment, she gave thanks to God and spoke about the child to all who were looking forward to the redemption of Jerusalem.' **Luke 2:36–38**

We're not sure what Anna's exact age was, but it is clear that she had been worshipping night and day, fasting and praying, for a very long time. Anna refused to be defined by the tragedy that she had experienced, but instead by prayerful expectation and devotion – she was a one-woman 24-7 Prayer Room!

Just as Simeon finished prophesying about the child in his arms, Anna joined them and gave thanks to God.

ASK

I ask myself, who am I grateful for? Who has encouraged me or comforted me or inspired me or challenged me to be a better me recently? Who would I like to give thanks to God for right now?

— Selah

Anna didn't just give thanks to God, but she spoke about the child, Jesus, to everyone she met. I ask You, God, to give me opportunities to spread the word and tell everyone I meet the good news about Jesus.

— Selah

YIELD

As I return to the passage, I open my ears to hear Your Word at a deeper level, and my heart to yield to Your will once again.

'There was also a prophet, Anna, the daughter of Penuel, of the tribe of Asher. She was very old; she had lived with her husband seven years after her marriage, and then she was a widow until she was eighty-four. She never left the temple but worshipped night and day, fasting and praying. Coming up to them at that very moment, she gave thanks to God and spoke about the child to all who were looking forward to the redemption of Jerusalem.' **Luke 2:36–38**

During this fourth and final full week of Advent, we've joined many of the main participants in the drama of Jesus' birth. We've sat on hillsides with shepherds, we've listened to the songs of angels, we've worshipped alongside wise men, and we've given thanks with Simeon and Anna in the temple. And as we've listened to their stories, we've also received our own invitation – the everlasting Advent invitation to come and meet Jesus for ourselves, once again. The 'good news of great joy' is that He is alive.

Jesus, I welcome You to be born, once again, into my life this Christmas. And at the same time, I receive Your welcome and I yield fully to Your invitation, to be born again into Your life too.

Closing Prayer

Father, may I live this day, true to You, come what may.
Jesus, may I give this day, in kindness to all, in every way.
Spirit, may I love this day, proclaiming Christ in all I say.
Amen.

DAY 29

We've been on the journey to Christmas and we've delighted in Jesus' coming. Now, as the season draws to a close, it births in us hope and expectation that He will come to us again…

One of the earliest recorded prayers of the Church is the Aramaic word *maranatha*, which literally means, 'Come, Lord Jesus'. The Latin word 'advent' means the same thing – 'come'. This is a season of waiting and wanting; looking and longing; inviting Christ to come once more into our lives and into our world. Pause now and repeat this ancient prayer several times slowly:

Maranatha, come, Lord Jesus.

— Selah

We're going to stick with this simple prayer, *Maranatha*, a bit longer.

If you are aware of sinful thoughts, words or deeds in your life, acknowledge them now before the Lord, praying: *Maranatha, come, Lord Jesus.*

— Selah

Now think of someone who needs Christ's love today, praying for them: *Maranatha, come, Lord Jesus.*

— Selah

Next, remember your own local church and the many activities it has planned during this Christmas season, praying again: *Maranatha, come, Lord Jesus.*

— Selah

Finally, think of a place in the world that desperately needs Christ's comfort today, praying: *Maranatha, come, Lord Jesus.*

— Selah

In the twelfth century, Saint Bernard of Clairvaux, a forerunner of the Cistercian order of monks, notably said that Christ comes three times: in the past to Bethlehem at Christmas, in the future at the end of the age, and in the present day lives of believers. Let's pray for all three:

> *Thank You, Father, for loving us so much that You sent Your Son*
> *to save us.*
> *Maranatha. May Jesus be born again among us this Christmas.*
> *Thank You, Jesus, that You came before and You are coming*
> *again in glory.*
> *Maranatha. We long for You to return and make all things new.*
> *Thank You, Holy Spirit, for filling my life.*
> *Maranatha. May the Lord Jesus Christ be born again in me today.*

Blessing

May this day bring Sabbath rest to your heart and your home.
May your peace and perspective be renewed in the busyness of this season.
May your hand be free enough from spending and acquiring to receive God's gift.
May a little of the wonder of Christmas awaken the child within today.
May God's Word feed you and His Spirit lead you into the week and into the life to come.

DAY 30: EXAMEN

We are almost at the end of another year.

PAUSE

I pause now, breathe deeply, and re-centre my scattered senses on the presence of God.

— Selah

Lord, in this busy season, please help me to be still. I am opening my ears now to hear amazing things from You, quietly preparing my heart for the wonder of meeting with You.

REJOICE and REFLECT

Today we're doing something a little different. Rather than reflecting on a passage from the Bible, we're going to reflect on our journey over the past twelve months and ask ourselves, how has God been with us throughout this year?

Together, we're going to adapt an ancient form of prayer called the Examen, and invite the Holy Spirit to remind us of the highs and lows of the year and reveal to us God's presence throughout.

I take a moment now to still myself in God's presence. I deliberately quiet my inner world.
I notice my thoughts – are they noisy or quiet? What's vying for attention? I offer my thoughts to God.

— Selah

I notice how I'm feeling – peaceful, excited, stressed, sad, something else? I offer my feelings to God.

— Selah

I notice my body – how do my muscles feel? Is my breathing shallow or deep? As I breathe deeply, I offer my body to God.

— Selah

*Holy Spirit, I welcome You. Guide me as I examine my year.
I take a moment to think back over the year. As I recall specific events
and people I take time to thank God for each one.*

— Selah

*As I think through each month, acknowledging the good times as
well as the more painful or challenging moments, I notice how I feel
reflecting back on them.*

— Selah

*Holy Spirit, bring to mind the ways I have sinned and fallen short this
year. I ask Your forgiveness.*

— Selah

*I ask You, Holy Spirit, to show me how You were in, over and through
everything I experienced this year. Remind me of the significant things
You have said and the Scriptures that have shaped my life.*

— Selah

ASK

*What from this year do I want to leave behind? I ask You, God, to help
me throw off everything that could hinder me from fully entering into
Your plans in the year to come.*

— Selah

*What are the things from this year that I want to take with me? Please,
Lord, help me to hold onto these things as I step into the New Year.*

YIELD

I make the words of this psalm my prayer today:

'Search me, God, and know my heart;
test me and know my anxious thoughts.
See if there is any offensive way in me,
and lead me in the way everlasting.' **Psalm 139:23–24**

Closing Prayer

Father, may I live this year, true to You, come what may.
Jesus, may I give this year, in kindness to all, in every way.
Spirit, may I love this year, proclaiming Christ in all I say.
Amen.

DAY 31

It's the final day of our Advent journey together.

PAUSE

I pause now, breathe deeply, and re-centre my scattered senses on the presence of God.

— Selah

Lord, in this busy season, please help me to be still. I am opening my ears now to hear amazing things from You, quietly preparing my heart for the wonder of meeting with You.

REJOICE and REFLECT

As you read and reflect today, consider writing down some of your thoughts, and the things that you hear from God.

I began my end of year 'examen' yesterday by reviewing this year, acknowledging the good times – the successes and achievements, the memorable moments – as well as the less-good times, and by becoming aware of God's presence in, over and through them all.

I am grateful for the year that has passed. Today, I am looking forward to the next.

In his letter to the Philippian church, Paul writes: 'But one thing I do: forgetting what is behind and straining toward what is ahead, I press on...' (Phil. 3:13–14).

The writer to the Hebrews uses similar imagery: 'let us throw off everything that hinders and the sin that so easily entangles. And let us run with perseverance the race marked out for us, fixing our eyes on Jesus' (Heb. 12:1–2).

ASK

As I think about the year ahead, what has been 'marked out' for this season of my race? What will I be doing in the year to come? What events will affect me? What changes will take place? As I think about these things, I notice how I feel about them.

— Selah

Yesterday, I identified some things that I want to carry from this year into next – lessons learnt, skills gained, relationships formed, seeds sown that I want to grow. How can I make sure that these seeds fall into good soil in my life – how can I give them room to grow?

— Selah

Lord, what are You speaking to me about for the year ahead?
Is there are verse or a story from the Bible that You're giving to me for the next twelve months?
Lord, what are You asking from me this year? Is there a new discipline that You are leading me into?

— Selah

YIELD

Jesus, I lay everything about the coming year before You. I fix my eyes on You alone. You are the author and perfecter of my faith – I yield to the story that You are writing in and through my life.

Closing Prayer

Father, may I live next year, true to You, come what may.

Jesus, may I give next year, in kindness to all, in every way.

Spirit, may I love next year, proclaiming Christ in all I say.

Amen.

Week One: Journeying with Elizabeth and Zechariah

We can often skip past the story of Elizabeth and Zechariah and jump right in to the miracle of Jesus' birth – but journeying with this ordinary couple, we meet individuals devoted, passionate and willing to follow God. The journey to the birth of John the Baptist shows how God can bring miraculous transformation when we encounter Him.

Read
Luke 1:5–24,57–65

Discuss
1. What's the longest journey you've ever been on? Was it enjoyable, or challenging?
2. The story begins by sharing Elizabeth and Zechariah's reputations and ancestry. Why do you think Luke introduces them in this way?
3. In just a few verses, we see a complete transformation of Elizabeth and Zechariah's situation. How do these verses encourage you?
4. Imagine you were in Zechariah's position. How would you have reacted to encountering an angel? What sort of questions would you have asked?
5. Have you ever experienced God intervening in your life in a miraculous way? Share your stories together.
6. When John is born, the whole community sees what God has done in the lives of Elizabeth and Zechariah. How do you want your community to encounter God's presence? Share your hopes and prayers together.

Pause
Invite the Holy Spirit to reveal one thing for you to remember from this week's study.

Rejoice and Reflect

What are you grateful to God for this week?
Are there situations where you're waiting to see God's breakthrough?
Or situations where you're feeling disappointed by God?

Ask

Together, pray for God's presence in the difficult, disappointing situations of life. Ask God to bring miraculous encounter.

Yield

Together, realign and devote yourselves to God, praising Him for His unending love and the miraculous gift of Jesus.

Week Two: Journeying with Mary

Mary's encounter with an angel is one of the most famous passages in the Bible. Yet from the moment Mary is chosen by God, she is encouraged and equipped for her role, and responds in adoration and praise. Mary's journey demonstrates to us that God is always present, and we are always able to encounter His presence in praise.

Read

Luke 1:26–56

Discuss

1. Has anyone shared something completely unexpected with you? How did you respond?
2. Throughout the Bible, God speaks in so many different ways – through signs, dreams, an audible voice. Why do you think God chose to send an angel to share this news with Mary?
3. What does the angel tell us about who Jesus will be? How is this similar or different to what is prophesied about Jesus?

4. Mary learns that her cousin has also experienced the miraculous power of God. How do you think this changes her perspective?
5. Mary and Elizabeth encourage one another. Who or what encourages you to keep going in your journey with God?
6. Mary's song of praise is a powerful response to God. How often do you stop to give thanks to God? Are there places in your life where you could cultivate an attitude of praise?

Pause

Invite the Holy Spirit to reveal one thing for you to remember from this week's study. *Listen, hear, obey.*

Rejoice and Reflect

What are you grateful to God for this week?
What task or role is God asking you to do at this time? How is God bringing encouragement, or empowering you to do what He's asking?

Ask

Together, pray for a fresh sense of encouragement in your individual journeys and tasks. Ask God to equip you for what's ahead.

Yield

Together, devote yourself to the plans that God has for each person and focus on Him.

Week Three: Journeying with Joseph

Joseph is often seen on the fringes of the Christmas story, forgotten or ignored in favour of the others at the heart of the action. But in the short verses we read about Joseph, his journey is full of purpose and identity. We can learn from Joseph to be certain that we have a clear part in God's story.

Read
Matthew 1:18–25; Luke 2:4–7

Discuss
1. What's the hardest decision you've ever had to make? What helped you make your choice?
2. In Mary and Joseph's context, a woman could be stoned for committing adultery (even when a couple were engaged). What's counter-cultural about Joseph's character? What would the equivalent reaction be today?
3. Joseph's dream led to a complete change of response, and he immediately obeyed God. Has God ever spoken to you through a dream? How confident did you / would you feel in taking action?
4. Joseph obeyed what God had said, but it was risky to go against society's laws and cultural habits. What can we learn from Joseph's choices to obey God?
5. Immanuel is a significant name of Jesus, meaning 'God with us'. What does the reality of 'God with us' look like for you in your daily life?
6. Because of Joseph's ancestry, Jesus was born in the place that was prophesied – Joseph was an integral part of God's story even though he wasn't at the centre of the action. In which places might you be an integral part of God's story?

Pause
Invite the Holy Spirit to reveal one thing for you to remember from this week's study.

Rejoice and Reflect
What are you grateful to God for this week?
Are there situations where God is challenging you to step out in faith?
Or are there places where you're not sure what your role is?

Ask

Together, ask God for courage and wisdom for the situations you're facing that are challenging or confusing.

Yield

Together, speak words of encouragement over one another and focus on your Christ-given identity.

Week Four: Journeying to Jesus

For the shepherds and Magi, their journey to Jesus wasn't easy – or even intentional. From these unlikely characters we meet in the Christmas story, we can learn what occurs when we step out of our routines to seek Jesus, and the incredible transformation when we encounter Him in worship.

Read

Luke 2:8–20; Matthew 2:1–12

Discuss

1. What's the best gift you've ever bought for someone? What was it? Why was it the best?
2. Why do you think the shepherds were some of the first people to hear about the birth of Jesus? What does this reveal about God's character?
3. The word 'Magi' comes from the same origin as the words 'magician', 'sorcerer' and 'astrologer'. Does this change your perception of them? How do you think their encounter with Jesus affected them?
4. Across both of these passages, there are multiple references to praise and worship – you might like to list them. How is the style and content of praise and worship similar or different to your praise and worship of Jesus?

5. The shepherds and Magi stepped out of their routines and made sacrifices to seek and worship Jesus. Do you think that Christians today have the same attitude? Why or why not?

6. We don't hear about the shepherds or Magi again, but we know that their brief encounters with Jesus were characterised by worship. How can we take our worship encounters with Jesus into our daily routines?

Pause
Invite the Holy Spirit to reveal one thing for you to remember from this week's study.

Rejoice and Reflect
What are you grateful to God for this week?
When in the rhythm of your life do you seek Jesus in worship? What other activity can you sacrifice, to spend time in His presence over Christmas?

Ask
Together, you might like to invite God to interrupt your regular routines. Ask God to give you a renewed passion and focus for worship.

Yield
Finish your time together in worship – by giving thanks for the gift of Jesus and the blessings that you've experienced. You might like to each specifically choose something to praise God for.

Continue your journey throughout 2020...

CWR and 24-7 Prayer have been working together to create a brand-new devotional app to help people engage with the Bible through prayer, reading and meditating on Scripture. Together we want to re-ignite the lost art of the 'quiet time' by putting a daily devotional resource in the hands of 18–25-year-olds that helps them understand, apply and prayerfully live out what they read in the Bible each day.

This will be available from the beginning of 2020, so if you've enjoyed the style and approach of this Advent book, please encourage friends and family to check out this new digital resource from CWR and 24-7 Prayer.

24-7prayer.com/dailydevotional

Journey to the cross next Lent...

Over six studies, Michael Baughen guides us through Paul's letters to the Corinthians, which show us how to go against the flow of selfish living and embrace what it means to suffer for Christ. Discover how Paul's teaching is just as important for Christians today as it was for the Early Church.

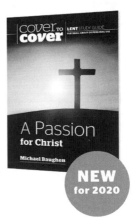

Author: Michael Baughen
ISBN: 978-1-78259-936-4

For latest prices and to order, visit **cwr.org.uk/shop** or call **01252 784700**